SPARROW TREE

Gwyneth Lewis was Wales's National Poet from 2005 to 2006, the first writer to be given the Welsh laureateship. Her first six books of poetry in Welsh and English were followed by *Chaotic Angels* (Bloodaxe Books, 2005), which brings together the poems from her three English collections, *Parables & Faxes*, *Zero Gravity* and *Keeping Mum*. Her latest poetry books are *A Hospital Odyssey* (2010) and *Sparrow Tree* (2011), both from Bloodaxe.

Her first collection in English, *Parables & Faxes* (Bloodaxe Books, 1995), won the Aldeburgh Poetry Festival Prize and was shortlisted for the Forward Prize for Best First Collection. Her second, *Zero Gravity* (Bloodaxe Books, 1998), was shortlisted for the Forward Prize for Poetry. The BBC made a documentary of *Zero Gravity*, inspired by her astronaut cousin's voyage to repair the Hubble Space Telescope. Both *Zero Gravity* and *Keeping Mum* (Bloodaxe Books, 2003) were Poetry Book Society Recommendations. *Y Llofrudd Iaith* (Barddas, 1999) won the Welsh Arts Council Book of the Year Prize and *Keeping Mum* was shortlisted for the same prize. In 2010 she won a Cholmondeley Award. *Sparrow Tree* won the Roland Mathias Poetry Award (Wales Book of the Year) in 2012.

Gwyneth Lewis composed the words on the front of Cardiff's Wales Millennium Centre. Her other books include *Sunbathing in the Rain: A Cheerful Book on Depression* (Harper Perennial, 2002), shortlisted for the Mind Book of the Year; *Two in a Boat* (Fourth Estate, 2005), which recounts a voyage made with her husband on a small boat from Cardiff to North Africa; and *The Meat Tree: New stories from the Mabinogion* (Seren, 2010).

She is a librettist and has written two chamber operas for children, *Redflight/Barcud*, with music by Richard Chew, and *Dolffin*, with music by Julian Phillips. She has also written an oratorio, *The Most Beautiful Man from the Sea*, to music by Orlando Gough and Richard Chew. All were commissioned and performed by Welsh National Opera with amateur singers. Her first stage play, *Clytemnestra*, was premièred at Sherman Cymru in 2012.

GWYNETH LEWIS

SPARROW
TREE

BLOODAXE BOOKS

For Leighton

ACKNOWLEDGEMENTS

Many of these poems were written while I was a Fellow at the Radcliffe Institute for Advanced Study at Harvard University, others while I was a Fellow at the Stanford Humanities Center. I'm deeply grateful to both institutions.

'Glaucoma' was commissioned by the Calouste Gulbenkian Foundation for the anthology *Signs and Humours*, ed. Lavinia Greenlaw (2007). 'How to Knit a Poem' was part of four programmes commissioned by BBC Radio 4 and produced by Penny Arnold. 'Prayer for Horizon' was commissioned by BBC Radio 3's *The Verb*, 'Spectrum' by the Dean and Chapter of St Paul's Cathedral for the Advent Procession 2005. An earlier version of 'Voice' was commissioned by the Shell BBC Singer of the Year competition 2008.

Some of these poems have appeared in *Agenda, Harvard Divinity Bulletin, Harvard Review, Michigan Quarterly Review, New Welsh Review, PN Review, Poetry Review, Salamander, Times Literary Supplement* and *The Tower*.

I owe the individual poem titles of 'Quilting for Childless Women' to *Amish Abstractions: Quilts from the Collection of Faith and Stephen Brown*, exhibited at the de Young Museum, San Francisco.

CONTENTS

SYRINX

Sparrow Tree

I had this tree
Where sparrows nested,
My aviary.

I welcomed a blackbird,
Which was wrong. That,
A better class of song
Went calling on the sparrows' nest.
Guess the rest.
You think I've blackbirds? They moved on
To kill elsewhere.

No tune, no subject.
Yes, imaginary birds,
But they're no use.
So, start again
With thorns, an invitation.

Taxonomy

Dusky junco, dusky junco, jay,
Towhee, testy towhee, testy towhee go
Swallow, swallow, swallow, swift,
Culture, give me cultured kite. Oh no,
The butcher bird. No! Not the shrike!
I will do, maybe, phalarope.
Ee, ah, oo, oh, oriole.

Field Guide to Dementia

To see you is egret,
No, red kite high
On a thermal,
Holding your hand
Is wagtail, comfort.

I think some cuckoo's laid
An egg of darkness in my head.

Words have migrated,
I forget their calls.

But I still point,
Look! Dowitcher, possibly
Lapwing. Quite.

Guest

A blue tit pecks at the window pane
Of your eye. It shatters, letting bird explode
In stars and auras on your retinal veins
Then up the optical nerve to your brain,
Like an idea. Painful, no doubt.
Me, I'd not want my visitor out.

What Do Birds Say?

Friday, a sparrow cried:
'Me! Me!'
That was difficult.

Saturday it was: 'You!'
I liked this no better.

On Sunday I heard
The sparrow say,
'We!' Bird and I
Enfolded together:

Syrinx, logos, feather, cry.

Murmuration

I fell among starlings,
Birds of the damned.

I understand myself to be single,
A rebel. I'm off!

They catch me,
Filing to magnetic field,
Fireless smoke.
Sighing, like electricity,
We settle on our chosen tree,
Bloody with berries.

I tell you, we had
That bush by the throat.

Birder

(i.m. my aunt Megan 1924-2009)

I

Midwinter, season for seeing through
Time and space. Before the War,
You were 'sparrow'. Now I hear
Geese in your breathing, oboe sighs.
Overhead they're leaving too. Each bird's
A letter, making sense
For a moment, then not. Cirrus of snow
Lays over the woods. Sluggish
With ice, the creek's pulse slows.

II

Morning performance on the stage
Under the feeder. Enter wild turkeys,
A *corps de ballet* in copper tutus.
Solo of startle – *entrechat, entrechat,*
Pas de bourrées – then the tom
Leads off his harem, one by one,
No curtsey, no curtain call. Then gone.

III

Fashion show: a black-eyed junco
Models its species – train,
Down jacket (in white and slate),
Then profile. When I die
I want to hear birds ricochet
Outside my window, feel the strobe
Of small flocks feeding. I'd like
To deserve this litany:
Woodpecker, waxwing, chickadee.

IV

It's no small thing to have lived your life
In cardinals' and tree-creepers' eyes.
They'll feel you first as a rendezvous missed,
Then hunger. Your body's the birds
Waiting as they rise and scatter
To a final slam of the kitchen door.

Virgin

1

You can't save me. I
Want hummingbirds.

My heart's a fountain
Attracting jays
Which jeer and bicker.

I want to be seen
By a vicious eye –
Beak's needle
In the quantum blur
Of iridescence.

That's it! There!

2

(Yawn) once
You don't need them,
They're everywhere.

LOGOS

Small Brown Job

May you be led on all your walks
By an unidentified bird
Flitting ahead, at least one branch,
The tease, between you
And it. Is that an eye-
Stripe? Epaulette? Your desire
For a name grows stronger.
Chaffinch? Warbler? This is spinning
Gold from straw. You're in good hands.
Shut up and follow.

Love Poem

I want to be as close to you
as the name *San Juan de Aznalfarache*
when you struggle to say it. A tune in the head
you can't forget. A name
full of vitamins. A word so rich
that I catch in your fillings. A rhythm,
a taste. A place
where, once, a poet was king
of Mudejar origin. *San Juan
de Aznalfarache. San
Juan de Aznalfarache.* Stumble,
stutter me before moving on
to the African citadels. Make your tongue
touch, ever so gently, the back of your teeth.
No. Let me show you. Like this.

Splinter

(for Finnley, aged 3)

In years to come, they will lodge in his heart.
I won't be me with a sterilised pin
Dislodging dashes of wooden rain
Aslant in his sole. He says it doesn't hurt,
I don't believe him. One fragment's stubborn.
Dig deeper. If I were a mosquito
I'd anaesthetise his novice skin
Before each stab. And then I'd suck
With more conviction and no less zeal
Than Helen, mother of Constantine,
Who scoured the length and breadth of Christendom
For a piece of the real cross.
Got it! Kiss his reliquary skin.

Imaginary Walks in Istanbul

1

It's time I made my daily promenade
to nowhere special – round the footstool
and parlour. Just as Søren Kierkegaard

and father took imaginary strolls
inside looking out, not needing travel.
I apologise now to Istanbul –

never been there – but I find myself full
of mosques and ferries, crosses and crusades,
a journey that's purely fictional.

I've drunk cool sherbert and lemonade
in Bosphorus villas: quarters of mind.
Untaken photographs will never fade

because they're unreal. I want a dervish,
Neck broken, to spin like a radar dish.

2

Let's start with omphalos, the empire's O
In Hagia Sophia, a porphyry
Belly-button that was Justinian's throne.

(Ignore Anonymous of Banduri
On the marble columns, he's full of shit.)
Upstairs, Christ holds a digital TV

Like legal tablets. Notice that he squints,
One eye on me, one on eternity
And he won't stop looking, so that I split

Apart like an atom. From out the frieze
Birds fly, wings bladed, the doorways' veils
Are torn to shreds by the slasher breeze,

A cathedral apocalypse: vermeil
And glass chandeliers explode to shrapnel.

3

The hidden contents of the ottoman.
We could slide down its armrest, and we did,
Often, its dark brown Victorian oilskin

Was slippery enough – I'd bump my head
Each time. In other moods, I'd count and thumb
The rosary of upholstery studs

Along the edge. By now you know that I'm
A counter, and I do admire a square
With something in it. My buttocks would numb

If I read on it – no give in horsehair
So thin. But the syllables from the east
Intrigued me. I loved this backless chair,

A hard place, not designed for rest.
My whole life's secreted inside this chest.

4

The Great Ones left evidence everywhere:
Not far from the Halberdiers-with-Tresses
You'll find a casket containing the hair

Of the Prophet Muhammed. You may gaze
On his tooth, his footprint, admire the hem
Of the Holy Mantle. The guidebook says

That the delightful Circumcision Room
Is not to be missed – go back if it's full.
Check out the Saucepan of Ibrahim.

What's 'like the apple but not the apple?'
A pear? Ram's testicles. Look how the crease
Between sweetbreads is perfect, the pouches full

Of goodness. Each night leaves a cicatrice
On my face. By day, it heals without trace.

5

A language in which the point of the i
Is optional must be admired. I rate
Such subtlety – the disposed-of housefly,

The cauterised mole. I hallucinate
ts without crosses (not the same as l).
You can count me out of the caliphate

That's coming. Not because I'm infidel
But my fid is other and my style
Non-fanatic. My headquarters are smell,

Rotting melon. Goat shit's a spiritual
Discipline if your dogma's maggots,
From whose prophetic writhings one might tell

Who goes to hell, who doesn't. High carrots
And lilies ooze tea. I believe those dots.

6

Last turn's to the Church of Constantine Lips,
which had seven apses and three narthex,
most unusual. Like the brain's lop-

sided map of the body: monstrous sex,
slight neck, a set of negligible limbs,
spatula fingertips – the practical codex

of how life feels. In the park by Taksim
Square: 'Madame, I am not a cannibal,
I merely wish to sell you a kilim

from my native province.' And, like a fool,
I let him. There are no silent letters
in Turkish, and he was so affable…

My tours, you'll note, have contained no errors
But getting lost is what guidebooks are for.

FEATHER

Quilting for Childless Women
(for Bob and Brenda)

1 *Pine Trees (Crib Quilt)*

First, bury ideas of a baby,
Then cover the hill
In juniper, laurel.

Imagine a lake
That doubles the view
Of desolation –

Tumulus twice.
Except that I've hidden
Waxwings and siskin,

Behind pine needles,
Feeding on insects and screaming
With exhilaration.

2 *Broken Plates*

I'm the child who played with glass,
A mirror jigsaw with pieces missing.
The proof? I've scars. Here, catch a glimpse
Of my desperate younger self with shard
Flashing an SOS so bright,
So urgent, it blinds me now with migraine.

3 *Tumbling Blocks*

The world insists on dazzle, jazz.
I've missed my tune, failed to hit the beat.
Each monthly scarlet could have been
A different person. Now I'm left with auras –
Flash foetuses – then pain
Stabbing, a dagger through the eye.
How will I ever know now
Where is the One of rhythm?
            Or the many of
Syncopation?

Not to have children's to be unrhymed,
Undeclined, more complete than you'd really like
At the end, when you're finally done
With your body and have to give it back,
Plus wear and tear. But, if we're immortal,
Even the childless will live for ever. If words
Are the cry of a baby for its absent mother,
Why mayn't I answer? I have milk to offer.

5 *Broken Star*

I lie down in a supernova,
Temperatures unknown to man
And sweat it out.
A person can't sleep
If her feet are cold.
I'm egg-yolk yellow, red and green,
An unusual sunset. Here's the thing: the more
You move towards infrared
The more you arrive where you started.

6 *Triangles*

Than which nothing's more painful
To believe that your own mother
Sees you as rival. Me, him, her.
She, me, it. Now I turn
To stitching shapes beneath this pattern,
A subtext of paisley and flourishes.
I manage, of course, to prick my finger
Through sixty thicknesses of cotton and silk.

7 *Double Wedding Ring*
(for H.W.)

The breakdown led to the need for a job,
That to a kitchen where he was baker
Teasing me about baggy jeans,
Which led to drinks – no pints for a girl,
Two halves. The thought of a possible affair
Which led to an awkward half-hour in the car
Then to life-long friendship. Call in, say hello
To mother and father, visit all three
When home. Partners presented for vetting,
Two weddings, then mutual visits,
Fond photos then a sudden death,
Look out for widow, continue to visit
Parents, Victoria sponge and tea –
Still cup and saucer after all these years –
Cry for the dead and laugh with the living,
So I'm hanging on now to a ringing phone,
No answer, ring-ring, ring-ring, next thing.

8 *Log Cabin, Barn Raising Variation (Crib Quilt)*

So resurrection's required
Again today. Earrings in lobes.
Smile on face. Raise high
The whatever. These people insist on hope
In all areas. Tight dovetails and architraves
(Remember to leave a hole for the smoke).
Me? I'm the pagan light outside
Disastrous liaisons of termite with oak.

9 Ocean Waves

(for A.J.)

X marks the spot where the body went under
The Channel's quilt, whose mighty tides
Rise twice a day. X marks a fetch

As language keeps coming but not the words
For X who was ours but is forever now
Anonymous, and X is how

The surge is lifted by the nursemaid moon
So earth can turn under it, an invalid rolled
Beneath a coverlet. X for the pain

We never located but would have exchanged
For Stay, Be Patient and We Understand
Though we didn't and, finally, X is the link

Of pressure with weather, a final lack
So utter that the slap and suck
Of water was better. Kiss-kiss, kiss-kiss.

I'm closed-up door, a No Through Road,
Head of a valley. But I have views
As far back as Ypres. Except for you,
None will look through me. To be
Always be child and never mother.
No exit. Time-lapse of a rotting rose.

11 *Crosses and Losses*

A park keeper called the garden closed,
But nothing's finished. I dream of my men
In the arms of another woman
Who's better in bed. She keeps them all,
Despite my protests. She'll not release them,
Because she's time, takes everything –
Whore that she is – won't be refused.

So I'm fairy godmother, a crone.
What do I bring to the christening
Of children I love but who aren't my own?
A dark-matter sun. Not flashy,
But to be relied upon
When things fly apart. I've had
Several mothers and moral DNA
Is heritable as light, twice as strong.

How to Knit a Poem

1 *Hobby*

The whole thing starts with a single knot
And needles. Word and pen. Tie a loop
In nothing. Look at it. Cast on, repeat

The procedure till you have a line
That you can work with.
It's pattern made of relation alone.

Patience, the rhythm of empty bights
Create a fabric that can be worn,
If you're lucky, practised. Never too late

To catch dropped stitches, each hole a clue
To something that's bothering you.
I link mine with ribbons, pretend

I meant them to happen. You make a net
Of meaning to carry round
Mindfully, a puzzle in sound

For trains and terrible waiting rooms.
Thought in action, it redeems
Odd corners of disposable time,

Making them fashion. It's the kind of work
That keeps you together. The armpit's tight,
But tell me honestly: How do I look?

2 *Aran*

Glaucoma won't let my mother knit:
fine wool's a problem, her most intricate stitch

unviable. Unravelling doesn't require sight.
Look into her eyeball and you'll see light-

receptor stars. Ganglion cells die,
darken the startling supernovae,

surprising eclipses for others to see
with their intimate, sighted jelly.

Each coastal village had a different style
of fisherman's sweater. The tide

reads blackberry stitch like Braille
with dexterous pressure, untangling the wool

of tendons. Tears are a retreating sea
full of dark fish swimming. Knit one, purl three.

3 *Late Starter*

I said: 'I want to learn to knit again
As an adult.' My mother replied:
'You'll never want to wear
Any sweater you finish.'

I pressed: 'I want that matrilineal ache
In wrists and knuckles, the honest work
That links generations, from Mam-gu's
Arthritic fingers, through to me.'
She insisted: 'It will give you RSI.'

'But *you* had to learn.' 'The war
Was boring. They made me wear
A Welsh-wool vest that prickled and itched.'
'Let's make it in cashmere.'
'No. Show me your practice square.'

I'll admit it was ropey – there were
Holes and loosness. With a frown
She tore back my sampler to a ball
Of perfect but useless potential.

Mary takes me in hand,
Casts on pink acrylic. 'Just make a start!
Hand-made dishcloths are all the rage!
The worst mistakes produce the best art!'

4 *Tension Square*

I grit my teeth and knit my stitches tight,
Astringent wales block out light.
I use my craft to help me ruminate
On enemies – this betrayer, that ingrate –
Resentments I guard and cultivate
Till I'm so practised in the art of spite
My needles spark and I ignite
The kindling yarn. My lap's a grate
Of hatred: '*She* was wrong, *she* was wrong. *I* was right.
She was *wrong*, she was *wrong*. I was *right*!'

5 *Heroine*

'All art requires self-sacrifice.
On behalf of our village I now retire to bed
For the worst of the winter. Next to my skin
Are the silkworm cocoons that I'll keep warm
While others are working in the frozen fields
Or gathering firewood. My dreams
Will give the village finest threads
For our famous white knitting, which we exchange
For seeds and supplies. It doesn't look hard,
But you try lolling for months on end,
No conjugal visits, in case my man
Crushes the cargo that I hold
Between cleavage and flannel. I was always good
In pyjamas and, yes, I'll get bored.
Doing nothing's a gift that I possess
Completely. It takes guts
To retire and lie, completely still.
It's a question of talent, and I
Have got what it takes. I'd never shirk –
No, don't thank me – this terrible work.'

6 *The Symbolism of Ancient Sweaters*

Homemade sweaters contain a code
To be read by initiates. This bobbling here's
A marriage proposal, the Fair-Isle cuff
Says: 'The dog is a spy. Meet me in town
On Tuesday.' Even more arcane
Are garments made by knitting machine.
I once had a sweater that must have declared:
'I only like men with facial hair.' They came.
The way you knit is how you make love,
How you are with your God.
It's a question of soul, of daily repair.
If space is made of superstrings,
Then God's a knitter, everything
Is craft, and perhaps we could darn
Tears in the space-time continuum.

7 *Fractals*

A Spanish marina. Loops of light
    Strobe sexily along a hull,
Bright skeins of water whose every bight
    I weave as mooring lines pull tight
With sighs against the panting tide.
I turn the scene and work the other side...

Here are bacteria whose folds
    Make startling patterns as they kill
Their hosts. And here are trendy moulds,
    E-coli mittens for the very skilled,
Strep so life-like that I clear my throat,
Sweat as I turn them inside out...

Revealing molecules in strings,
    Pretzel knots, chaotic braids.
I witness in awe atomic weddings
    As protons take electron brides
Then divorce. They twist and turn,
In love for ever. Reality, my favourite yarn.

8 *Hypnosis Knitting*

A day of wordless misery,
Thorns in the heart.

This pattern wants only rhythm from me:
No judging, no knowing,
Just moving on
Into a future.

My grandmother's craftwork,
I suddenly see,
Was self-medication.

I'm working three
Axes. First, a new personality
Made from patience.

Second, a scarf
Composed in calm,
A respite from my usual self-harm.

The third's my finest.
Look! I've unpicked
Myself from worry, a delicate stitch

Into the present. No one can see
This last. Mindfulness charges the air,
Arrays me in intricate gossamer.

Mine starts with ribbing made of rain
On circular needles, so that the sleeves,
When they wear out, can be replaced
Like choruses. I'll have shoes
For pockets, the soles worn out
From dancing. There'll be a Hall of Fame,
A panel in Aran with silhouettes
Of Milton, Herbert. I'd like a boat
In the story – if you can knit,
Splicing comes easy – and an aviary
Of all the birds I've never seen.
I'll have a computer linked to the eyes
Of Hawaiian telescopes, so I can view
The mottle of early nebulae,
Which were a feature of my work.
I'd like it to be a pleasure to wear,
Lush as a Moorish orange grove,
Soft as moss... I must start soon.
It's cooling and, as night comes on
Terrified, I hear soft whirrs:
The pollen-heavy moths of time.

CRY

Voice

This singer has swallowed
An animal. It's lodged,
Still struggling,
Stuck in her throat.
The belly takes
A couple of beats
To start up the bellows.
Alarmed, the lady's
Eyes look down
At the vibrato
Flexing her jaw.
Her daemon sings
If she wants it to
Or not. We clap
And cheer, demanding
More. We never,
Ever want it to stop.

'As Long as you Want'

Sappho, Fragment 45, tr. Anne Carson

1

I'll get out of bed, take a shower, dress,
If not in my favourite clothes, in second best,
Turn up for my life, even find joy
In unexpected petals on trees
Whose name I don't know but plan to learn.
I'll do it, if there's the slightest chance
You'll need me, say, at the end of a day
When the wind's hormonal. Don't decide
This second, I'm willing to wait. How long?
If I can survive the next half hour
With no face and no name – and I think I can –
I'm willing to write you a crisp blank cheque
On myself which I'll honour to the last penny.
For what in return? I was going to say
For the hope that you'll hear me, begin to turn
Towards me, but that isn't true. No,
I'll leave it entirely up to you.

2

The new leaf's task is to have ideas
Above itself. In dreams you appear
As people I know and sometimes hate,
Like the couple that caught me
Rushing through highly formal gardens
Over lawns where I'd no right to be
In order to reach a flowering cherry tree,
Run into its arms, pull down its blossoms
Into my face, reliving a particular day
Only we remember, and exactly why.

3

Don't make me beg. I don't even know
What I'm wanting, or what gave me the idea
You were my answer, but I know you are.
I ask for favours, you've given me none.
This is getting me nowhere. I plod
Like a horse to the end of the line,
Tilling the soil. Though this crop fail
I believe in the ploughing. Look up! Life falls
Like seed from the loving sky,
We live in blizzards of unseen snow.

Spectrum

Look to the dark, it's full of company,
Though dust obscure the birth of a star.
Waiting creates a wider way to see.

Galaxies breathe out their chemistry
In cosmic rays, which our bodies bear.
Look to the dark, it's full of company.

We're shipwrecked in a radio sea,
Swept by beams of lighthouse pulsars.
Waiting creates a wider way to see.

The heart obeys its own gravity,
But sight expands to light from afar.
Look to the dark, it's full of company.

The music of what's killing me
Is shifted red, so hard to hear.
Waiting creates a wider way to see.

Help me to live this blind energy
Until the moment my own death flares.
Look to the dark, it's full of company.
Waiting creates a wider way to see.

Remission Sevillanas

Now that you're with me, back from the dead
(I didn't turn round! I didn't
Turn round!) I'm losing my mind.
No loss, you say. Outside
Oranges ripen in cold
For bitter marmalade.

I thought you were gone. The Guadalquivir
Swells each day with a fifty-mile tide.
I saw you drifting on the evening ebb
In a tiny dinghy – no engine, no oars –
Under dark eucalyptus. I called till the herons flew
But you didn't hear me. Don't you know
The strength of the current? How the greedy sea
Takes everything to it? – dead horses, old shoes,
Tree trunks – how it never lets go,
No, not even at the furthest reach
Of Sanlúcar de Barrameda and the wrecking bar?

You say you can't dance,
But your blood cells can,
Lymphoma flamenco, full of passionate verve,
Technique and *duende*. Deep in the bone
You need a different rhythm now –
Uno, dos, tres, quatro, cinquo, seis –
No *tarantella*, but the writhe of a snake
Tuning the mesh of your DNA,
A Sevillanas, with viper hands,
Stamping on cancer.
Now's the fiesta. *Eso es. Ole.*

Prayer for Horizon

I wish you, first, an unimpeded view.
Somewhere to aim for but which retreats
As fast as you travel. It can be
Sensible, Rational, a welcome thread
To hold onto if you ever feel sick.

In fog, I wish you artificial horizon,
Mercury level, so that you grasp
Where not to be, quickly. I wish you the gift
Of knowing where your knowing ends.

And finally, I ask: when you reach
The event horizon from which your light
Will no longer reach me and space, highly curved,
Hides you for ever, that you watch me arrive –
You shouldn't see me, but you will –
Signals flashing as I glide
In a flotilla of full-rigged ceremonial ships
To the edge of your singularity
On acres of scintillating sea.

Sea Virus

I knew I should never have gone below
but I did, and the fug of bilges and wood
caught me aback. The sheets of my heart
snapped taut to breaking, as a gale
stronger than longing filled the sail
inside me. To be shot of land
and its wood smoke! To feel the keel
cold in a current! To see the mast
inscribing water like a restless pen
writing a fading wake! It's true,
I'm ruined. Not even peace will do
to keep me ashore now. Not even you.